Animals

ON

THE

by FEODOR ROJANKOVSKY

Alfred A. Knopf New York

This title was originally catalogued by the Library of Congress as follows:

Rojankovsky, Feodor, 1891–
    Animals on the farm. New York, Knopf ₍1967₎
      1 v. (chiefly col. illus.) 29 cm.

    1. Animal pictures.   ɪ. Title.

PZ10.R65Ao   j 636   67—18586
Library of Congress   ₍68f5₎

Trade Ed.: ISBN: 0- 394-81875-X   Lib. Ed.: ISBN: 0- 394-91875-4

THIS IS A BORZOI BOOK PUBLISHED BY ALFRED A. KNOPF, INC.

TO OUR ANIMAL FRIENDS

rooster

horses

mallard duck

goose

COWS

goats

bull

turkey

hen

ducks

pigs

stork

swans

rabbits

peacock

donkey

sheep

cats

dogs